DOWN FOR

THE COUNT

DOWN FOR
THE COUNT

Bouncing Back from
Life's
Blows

Volume III

Compiled by Felicia C. Lucas

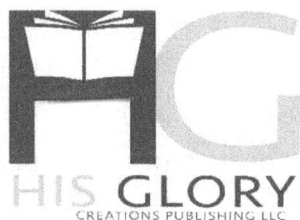

His Glory Creations Publishing, LLC
Wendell, North Carolina

TABLE OF CONTENTS

DEDICATION

This book is dedicated to individuals who are facing impossible situations and are seeking some inspiration in order to make it through the storm.

ACKNOWLEDGEMENTS

AUTHOR JANICE VICK

I would like to thank the Lord, Jesus Christ, for me reaching this phase in life. I would like to thank my family for supporting and encouraging me. There are some people who their support has been overwhelming in my life: Grady Walston, who has been my friend ever since I started playing for First Congregational church. The way you have supported me through the years has been wonderful. Secondly, Pastor Victor and First Lady Audrey Galloway. When I lost my mother suddenly in 2016, God placed you into my life. He knew I would need someone to fill the void that was left, and he filled it with you. You taught me that it's ok to express love for one another

Lastly, I would like to thank my two best friends, Todd Freeman and Iris Logan-Dickerson. You two mean more to me than you realize, and I will love you for life.

AUTHOR DR. ANGELA POWELL

I dedicate this book to my mom (Ida Downey, deceased,1940-2015), for praying me through hard times; to my son (Jonathan Powell), for always encouraging and being supportive to me. I thank Pastor Rod Parsley and Breakthrough Prayer Center for being available to take my suicidal call and minister to me.

Special thanks to my God's Army Prayer Warrior Prayer-Team for praying me through: Min. Rovella Watson, Min. Glen Supak, Min. Deborah Coleman, Pastor Lucinda Williams, and Min. Cheri Gallergher. A special thanks to my friend, Min. Diane Pace for encouraging me to write this book.

AUTHOR PAMELA HORNE

First, I give Glory, Honor and Praise to my Lord and Savior Jesus Christ. Thanks to my former Pastor and Aunt, the late Dr. Mae V. Horne, my parents Frank and Bessie Horne for raising me to believe in my abilities. To the late Al Wiggins, my favorite college professor who instilled in me confidence to write. Special thanks to Tina Thompson, who has been my biggest cheerleader. My Sissy, Daphne who continues to push, believe in and support. Thanks, Martin, for setting up my office and reminding me that I am supposed to write. Love to all my brothers, Frank, Thomas, Martin and Will; my sisters Melanie and Leanne and my big sister, the late Felecia Harris. Thanks to my cousin Jaqueline Barnes for purchasing the first copy of my first book. Thanks to the Women of Triumph, Pastor Marian Freeman-Weaver and the Gateway to Heaven UHC family and all those who supported me.

AUTHOR TINA MOORE

Thank you to my children and grandchildren for your support and encouragement. It will forever mean more than you could ever know. You guys are my reason, and I love each of you infinite. Mom, you are the best Mom EVER! Your love for me is amazing. You bring me joy, and I will always thank God for giving you to me. To my grandparents and uncles, may each of you continue to rest in heavenly peace. The roles you all played in raising me never went unnoticed, and I will forever shout you out. XOXO.

Finally, my dear friend Elizabeth Williams. Liz, thank you so much for believing in me, never switching up, and your weekly reminders about the greatness that is within me.

AUTHOR KIM MALLOY

First and foremost, thank you to our Heavenly Father that has been by my side since birth, leading me through things I didn't have a clue about in this world, to my spirit guides I believe were assigned to me from God, thank you for continuing to show me guidance towards reaching my full potential and fulfilling my life mission.

To my love Malik, thanks for showing me support through the process of becoming my best self.

To my clients that support me, thanks! To the two phenomenal leaders I met from AmplifyHer, Karen Gilliam and Felicia Lucas, thanks for the reassurance. To YOU reading my story thanks! I hope you gained insight to help you on your journey.

AUTHOR TRENA HINES

I want to humbly and graciously thank my Creator/ my God for giving me the opportunity to experience the beauty of life. Thank you to my pastor, Apostle Phillip A. Walker for being the true messenger of God. You told me that I had a testimony that someone needed to hear. God stirred the gift up in me to put it on paper. I also want to thank Andrea McCullough for being such a true friend.

Thank you, Diane Pace, for being supportive and encouraging through the years. Marie Hill, thanks for believing in me and helping me to believe in myself. Minister Felicia, I'm grateful to be a part of this phenomenal project. To my daughter Tamarah...The loving depth of your words made all the difference, and that was for me to see reality. Thank you, sweetheart!!!

AUTHOR ANNA LYONS

First, I give praises to God. Praise to my family, friends and members of Women of Triumph Ministry for supporting me. Thank you, Pastor Marian Freeman-Weaver and Gateway to Heaven United Holy Church, for your guidance and prayers. Thank you to the late Mae V. Horne, my spiritual advisor. To my Mentor Apostle Robert Johnson, thanks for your guidance and prayers. Thank you to my AmeriPlan family, Karl Ryans for encouraging me to write my chapter. He has taught me the importance of building financial wealth and leaving a legacy for my grandkids. Thank you to both my Publisher, Minister Felicia Lucas and Minister Diane Pace who played integral parts in inspiring me to utilize this gift of writing that God has given me. To my only child George Tisdale, thank you, son, for always believing in me and encouraging me to tell my testimony.

AUTHOR CONSTANCE HARRIS

I want to thank the love of my life, Elder John Harris, for his unwavering love and support of me. I also want to express my love to Cierra, Trey and Michael for being the best children a mom could ask for. I also thank my mother, Grace Ward, my late Father, Curtis Ward, along with my sisters, Veronica Womack and Candice Guest who were always my best cheerleaders. Also, I want to thank Gateway to Heaven UHC, my late Pastor, Dr. Mae V Horne along with my current pastor, Elder Marian Freeman-Weaver, for their spiritual guidance. And finally, a big shout out to The Women of Triumph Ministries, and CEO - Elder Anna Lyons, for being the best spiritual sisters and Mentor when I need them the most. To God be the Glory!!

AUTHOR FELICIA LUCAS

Thank you to my husband, children, family and friends who have consistently supported me on my literary journey. I appreciate each of you. To my spiritual mentor, Apostle Kim, thank you for praying for and with me.

To my co-authors, thank you for participating in this project and having the courage to share your stories. Each of you are phenomenal and I am so excited about this journey we are taking together!

To my His Glory Creations Publishing LLC team, thank you for everything! You are simply amazing!

CHAPTER 1

JANICE VICK

Janice Vick was born in New York but was raised by her two grandmothers, Bessie Morgan in Bailey, NC and Marie Vick in Middlesex, NC. At 5, she started playing the piano on her own. At 12, she played and led songs in the choir. Today she plays for multiple churches, leads praise teams, writes and composes music.

She is also passionate about fitness. One day, while looking through a muscle and fitness magazine, she came across Cory Everson and Lenda Murray, 20-time Ms. Olympia champions. When she saw their physiques, she instantly knew she wanted to be a bodybuilder.

She was on the right track until a diagnosis of lupus halted her journey. She is still on a quest to continue her dream of competing. Even though lupus has taken her out of the workforce, her desire is to become a personal trainer and coach. She wants to help others reach their fitness goals, inspire and encourage others to keep fighting and not give up.

YOU ARE CHOSEN

Commit everything you do to the Lord.
Trust him, and he will help you.
Psalms 37:5
New Living Translation

You are chosen! Those words were spoken to me by my former Pastor, Donald R. Ingram. Of course, at the time, I didn't understand what he meant. But when I think about it, maybe I understood, but I didn't believe it. I felt chosen people lived happy lives, not the life I lived. Honestly, to me my life didn't start out very well.

My very first memory was being abandoned by my mother, or what I thought was abandonment. After she married my stepfather when I was 5, they left for Delaware without me. I was her child, and she left me behind. My real father didn't take me with him when he moved to New Jersey. No one wanted me. Why

3

didn't my parents want me? Was I a bad child? Did I do something wrong? I could never understand. Later my mother told me that my grandmothers wouldn't let her take me. They wanted me to stay here. Why did they want me to stay here and not be with my parents? They never told me why. However, nevertheless they raised me and did the best they could.

I was mostly raised by my mother's mother. Understand she did her best, but she didn't exactly encourage me the right way. I guess the only way I can explain that statement is to give an example. When I was very young, I gave speeches in church. That's what our churches did back then. They held speech competitions and the church with the best speaker would win. Well, one day I was chosen to represent our church. Mind you, I had spoken several times and did very well. Well, this one time I go up to speak, and the church is packed. My heart starts beating fast, and I am nervous. I begin my speech, and I just forget my words right in the middle. I was so embarrassed I ran to my seat until the program was over, with my head hanging down. When we got into the car, instead of making me feel better, she called me stupid and dumb. "How could you embarrass me like that?" "You're so stupid." Then she got so mad she slapped me across the face. I knew then I could never be good enough for her. One of her favorites lines to me were, "Why can't you be more like Jennifer?" Jennifer was my very smart cousin. She got straight A's, studied hard and made my uncle and aunt very proud. My grandmother wanted me to be so much like her that I grew to dislike her. I know it's a terrible thing to say, but it's the truth. I got so tired of being compared to her. My grandmother isolated me. She wouldn't let me play much with the local kids, so I grew up a loner.

My school years weren't any better. I didn't know

how to socialize with other kids, and when I did, they would make fun of me. High school was the worst. I was called all kinds of names. I remember being called ugly and a giant because I was very tall. However, one name that still hurts me to this day was "grape ape." He was a cartoon character who was a giant ape. I loathe high school. I didn't have many friends until one day I met her. The girl that would become my best friend, Kathy McCalston. She and I became so close. She loved me dearly, and we hung out all the time. She was my lifesaver in high school. Unfortunately, after we graduated, we kind of lost touch. She got married and had children. I was in college, but one day out of the blue, she contacted me. My best friend was back in my life, but it wasn't for long. She was diagnosed with colon cancer, and she passed away. It still breaks my heart to this day. My one friend that truly loved me and she was gone.

As I said, my childhood wasn't great. I was hurt a lot. I was even hurt by a family friend who was supposed to love and protect me, but instead, he molested me. He abused me all through elementary school until I finally was able to get away from him when I went to junior high school. I don't want to spend too much time on this subject because it's a secret I have kept all my life. But it's safe to say that it affected me deeply. It contributed to me not being able to form meaningful relationships.

After high school, I went to college at NC State. It kind of started off the same with me being a loner. Not being comfortable around people and not able to form relationships. That is until I joined New Horizons choir. They were a gospel choir formed by two people who would have an enormous effect on my music future, Ron Foreman and Elaina Ward. I loved that choir. We treated each other like family. I felt safe and not judged. We sang all over North Carolina. I never wanted it to end, but sadly, it did. In January of 1990, I was in my apartment, and I received a call that my grandmother had collapsed at work and was taken to the hospital. I immediately drove to Wilson, NC. They ran tests and sent her home. About two weeks later, it happened again. This time we got a diagnosis. It was brain cancer. She had an orange-sized tumor on her brain from years of working in a tobacco factory. I didn't know what to do. My mother was in Delaware, and I had to take care of her until my mother came home. She was in and out of the hospital for six months. In June of 1990, she entered hospice care. I was alone at home with her. I was so scared. I didn't want to be alone in the house when she passed. I believe God knew that too.

Sunday morning June 10th, I wanted to go play at church, but I couldn't because no one would be there with her. I was sitting at home, and I heard a knock on the door. It was her brother. He told me to go to church and he would sit with her. I went to church and sat at the piano. We barely got through the opening hymn when the usher came up to me and told me to stop playing and walk outside. I walked outside and saw a lady from Bailey. I immediately knew my grandmother was gone. She died right after I left.

The person that took care of me, no matter how hard she was on me, she was gone. I felt lost. I didn't know what to do. I couldn't go back to school because I had no direction. I was all alone. So, I had to be taken care of by my father's mother, Marie. She was a wonderful woman but hard on me also. But they loved me. She passed away in 2013 from cancer. However, I thank God that I wasn't alone in the house when she passed away. God protected me both times from that kind of pain. He knew what effect it would have on me.

I could write an entire book on my life. The times God didn't allow Satan to destroy me. My diagnosis of lupus in 2006 was the heaviest. That was a head-scratcher. I didn't see that coming. I woke up to go to New Year's Eve service, and I can't walk. It took the doctors time to diagnose me and years to get stable. During those years, I fell into a deep depression and thought about suicide. I just wanted it to be over.

One Sunday morning, I was in bed, and I asked God to please take me. I said, "I'm ready to go." I didn't want to deal with that anymore. Moments later, my aunt enters my bedroom. She didn't say one word. She just got on her knees, prayed and then left. I began to get better. The doctors put me on a new medication. I started to gain weight and get stronger. Again, God didn't allow Satan to take me out, but he didn't give up. He figured he would attack what I loved to do, which is play the piano. I had six surgeries on my right hand. My one prayer request to God was to please don't allow Satan to steal my gift and he answered that prayer.

I guess the next heart-stopper was my mother's death. It was an 8am resurrection service and normally I would have gone home after service and been alone, but it so happened that the pastor and his wife invited me to spend the night with them that Saturday night so I wouldn't have to drive so far that morning. I went to the resurrection service, and it was good. God really used me that morning. We went back to the house and I got a message from my sister to call her. I called and she gave me the news that Mama was gone and that she had died that morning. I guess I screamed so loud that Pastor Galloway and Audrey came running in the room. I told them what happened, and they held me in their arms and cried with me. Then they followed me all the way back to Middlesex, just to make sure I was ok. I'm thankful for Pastor Victor Galloway and First lady Audrey Galloway. They have been such a blessing in my life. They hadn't even been at the church a year yet, and they took me into their lives. That's not even the church I belong to, and they treat me like I'm a member and a part of their family and I love them dearly.

I could go into so much...my being diagnosed with bipolar depression is a whole chapter itself. But God didn't allow Satan to take me out because I was chosen to be his vessel to serve him, and that's what I'm doing. God is not through with me yet.

CHAPTER 2

DR. ANGELA POWELL

Dr. Angela Powell is a decorated US Army Veteran. She teaches school in Granville County, NC. She's the CEO of "Arch Angel's Ministries Inc.," the Pastor of "Arch Angels International Deliverance Church," Producer of "The Power of Pray Warfare" TV broadcast and the Host of "The Victorious Women of Destiny" radio show.

She holds an Honorary Doctorate degree in Divinity from the Bible Institute of America. She completed her Chaplaincy Internship program of Clinical Pastoral Education with the Department of Veteran's Affairs in Durham, NC. She studied Evangelism with World Harvest Bible College, Demonology and Spiritual Warfare with Hosanna Bible College, Theology with the North Eastern Theological Institute. She currently, pursues a degree in Substance Abuse Counseling.

GOD DELIVERERED ME

I pray to you, LORD. I beg for mercy. I tell you all my worries and my troubles, and whenever I feel low, you are there to guide me. A trap has been hidden along my pathway. Even if you look, you won't see anyone who cares enough to walk beside me. There is no place to hide, and no one who really cares. I pray to you, LORD! You are my place of safety, and you are my choice in the land of the living. Please answer my prayer. I am completely helpless. Help! They are chasing me, and they are too strong. Rescue me from this prison, so I can praise your name. And when your people notice your wonderful kindness to me, they will rush to my side.
Psalm 142
Contemporary English Version

When I was a toddler, my mom lived with her Grandma. My Great-Grandma was a God-fearing woman, known as the Mother of her church. I was a happy, energetic child who loved to dance to the beat of tambourines and washboards in the church. It was during this time that my Great-Grandma proclaimed; I would be used by God. She spoke this during a time when my mother was in a great struggle to provide for me and my brother. She'd only been married for a couple years, when my father shot and killed his best friend. This resulted in him serving 5-years in prison. The first 5 years of my life, I was fatherless. My mom moved from place to place, surviving on family handouts with me on her hip and my brother at her side.

My dad's release from prison meant security for my mom. Finally, there was someone to provide and help raise her children. Unfortunately, after his release, all I can remember is the smell of alcohol, bloody fights and hiding in closets for fear that he would beat me the way he beat my mom. The tranquil days of living with my Great-Grandma were gone. I always looked forward to spending the night at her house and going to church with her. She called me kitten and she always made me feel so special and loved.

When I was 7, my parents decided to move out of North Carolina to get a fresh start in New York. After they got settled, my dad came back to pick us up for our move to New York. That was the first time I remembered being fondled. I didn't know if it was real or if it was a dream. (In 2014, one of my mom's sisters confessed that she remembered it happening to me at 6 years old, but I don't remember). When we moved to New York, the drinking and fighting between my parents became more frequent. I was always afraid that one day he would kill her. I remember crying and begging God to please send me back to live with my mother's mom or her grandma. The older I got, the more the fondling intensified, it occurred at night when everyone else was asleep and I was too afraid to tell anyone about what was happening to me. I prayed to God and cried most days. I even slept in my pants at night, as protection. I hated what my father was doing to me, and I was afraid to tell my mom, because I knew she was helpless to fight against him.

When I was around 11 years old, I felt filthy, nasty, dirty, ugly and I didn't want to go to school. I felt hopeless, all alone and I just wanted to disappear from that life. One day, instead of going to school, I went on top of our 4-story apartment building and I decided to jump off the roof. I went to the edge of the roof, crying hysterically as the sun shined down on my face. I remember stepping off the roof. But when I awakened, I was laying on the rooftop, away from the edge. It was nighttime and I could hear people talking. But when I got up and looked around, no one was there. I remember being disappointed, because I couldn't kill myself.

For he will order his angels to protect you
wherever you go
Psalm 91:11

I was 12 years old when we moved back to North Carolina. It was then that I found my voice and strength to say NO!! I finally told my mom and my father's mom, what Dad had been doing to me, but by that time, Dad had convinced them that I was a Fast-tail-hardheaded liar. By age 14, on a night when my mom was out with her friends, he succeeded in raping me. When I wiggled myself from under his alcoholic breath, I locked myself in our toilet chamber room, until mom came home. After this, he never touched me again, but we had a love/HATE relationship. I graduated from High School at age 17 and left home the same night. I left with a root of bitter, unforgiveness, rejection and rage.

I didn't know I was broken, until God fixed me!

When I was 21 years old, I joined the military, to run away from my past, but my past soon caught up with me. I was gang raped during boot camp and I almost lost my mind. After the rape, I was convinced that I deserved everything that happened to me. I could hear my father's voice calling me slut, whore, liar, and I believed he was right.

At 23 years old, I met a gentle, loving soldier, who asked me to marry him. Shortly after our marriage, during intimacy, I began to have flashbacks of my childhood and the rape. I could see my father's face during intimacy and all I could do was cry. I was on my job in Germany, when I broke down in tears and locked myself in the bathroom stall. I was ordered to seek counseling from the Military Chaplain. My husband and I also went to church and sought counseling from the Pastor. Every time I thought of giving up, God always placed me amongst his saints. Being in church around God's people always gave me peace, strength and hope. I didn't understand how much I needed God's Church. As soon as I'd feel better, I'd leave the church.

I believed I was healed from my past, until we took custody of my husband's baby nieces. Fear, anxiety and distrust reoccurred again. I was so overly protective of my girls. I didn't trust anyone. I was like a grizzly bear over her cubs. The flashbacks, bitterness and sadness came back again. We sought a Christian Family Therapist. In 1993, after 10 years of marriage, I lost my husband in a house fire and this was the turning point to my salvation. It was during this time; I tricked my father into going with me to one of my therapy sessions. For the first time ever, he admitted to molesting me. He apologized to me with tears of sorrow. It meant more than a world of counseling, to hear him say, "I'm sorry I did those things to you." I felt as light as a feather but limped as a rag. I received so much healing, just to hear him apologize.

In 1996, I lost temporary custody of my girls. Within 2 years I'd lost my husband, all my possessions and now my girls. The devil came back to me with thoughts of hopelessness and suicide. I sat on my bed with a bottle of liquor and my 9-millimeter weapon, flicking TV channels and contemplating suicide. I saw a preacher on TV named, Rod Parsley and he was talking about the love of Jesus. The word was so powerful that I couldn't turn the channel nor shut him out. I picked up my phone, as he had instructed, and I called The Breakthrough Prayer Center crying hysterically and asked for help. During that prayer call, I gave my life over to Jesus. And now, I know I can't survive without Jesus living through me. During the prayer, I went from uncontrollable crying to hysterical laughing and asking to speak in tongues. I had so much joy and peace, I felt like I was higher than the sky. God took away my bitterness and I could no longer find unforgiveness, hatred or rage in my heart. For the first time in a long time, I felt loved and I fell in love with Jesus. God gave me a brand-new heart filled with love and thanksgiving. Over the years, I've witnessed my mom, dad, sisters, brothers, uncles, aunts and cousins surrender their lives to Jesus. I no longer doubt who I am, because I know he's anointed me to destroy burdens, break yokes and set my people free. With His gift, I have power to break chains, destroy the darkness of drugs, alcohol, poverty and lunatic demons. God healed me from ovarian cancer, throat tumors, cysts on my bowels, depression, bitterness, unforgiveness and poverty. Most importantly, he's given me the power to cast out demons, lay hands on the sick and see them recover.

Everything the devil used to oppress me with, God used for His own Glory. I worked as a Prayer Warrior with the Breakthrough Prayer Center; where I'd been delivered from suicide. Now, I could pray for other suicidal victims and set them free. In 2006, I trained as a Counselor with the Women's Clinic of Columbus, under Pastor Rod Parsley. The training brought me through the darkest places of my own deliverance and prepared me to be an effective counselor. Now, I can encourage, God's confused daughters and give them hope in knowing that God has not forsaken them. I'm empowered to love, forgive and laugh.

CHAPTER 3

PAMELA HORNE

Elder Pamela Horne was born the fourth child of eight in Island County, Washington State. She was raised and educated in Durham, NC. A woman of God with a compassion for ministering to broken women, she has a heart for seeing men and women delivered, restored and renewed in Christ. In 1988, she earned a Bachelor's degree from Western Carolina University in Radio/TV and Journalism, a Bachelor's degree in Christian Education and Biblical Studies in 2011 from the Durham Extension of the United Christian College of Goldsboro, NC.

Elder Horne began her ministry under Pastor Dr. Mae V. Horne of Gateway to Heaven UHCA. She was ordained under Chief Apostle William D. Lee in 2012. In 2015, her vision for Consuming Fire Ministries was birthed. She continues her ministry work at Gateway to Heaven UHC. She recently retired from the Durham County Sheriff's Office (Detention Division) after over 27 years of service. Currently, she serves as the Co-Director and Event Planner of The Women of Triumph Ministries. She is a true worshipper and loves music & singing.

Connect with Pamela:

Facebook: Consuming Fire Book Ministries
Email: consumingfirebooks@gmail.com

THIS IS MY EXODUS

Then the Lord said to Moses, now you will see what I do to Pharoah: Because of my mighty hand, he will drive them out of his country."
Exodus 6:1

When you become a born-again Christian, you are delivered from bondage and rescued from the spirit of Egypt. Egypt is a place of rebellion and wickedness against God. Taskmasters carry out the bidding of the spirit of Pharoah.

The Egyptian kings or Pharaoh means the son of the sun. They were considered as gods and the name Pharaoh was synonymous with the destruction of good things in infancy. This spirit can manifest as a strongman or principal-demon controlling a person, family, place, or thing and bringing it under subjection to bondage. This spirit will never release a slave and will deprive them of freedom to reach their full potential for the Lord.

Like the Israelites enslaved in Egypt, I was bound to a job for over 27 years. 30 years and I would have reached full retirement, but God caused "the spirit of Pharoah" to drive me out. This is the story of my Exodus.

I was branded in the infancy of my career, ostracized, and hated without cause. I was also not saved. Eleven years later, when I gave my life to Christ, I stayed there to complete my assignment from the Lord. God positioned me in places throughout the rest of my career to minister to the "Israelites" still in bondage. Many began to seek the Lord as God instructed me to pray. Sometimes, God instructed me to fast along with prayer. I remember occasions where I had to fast three days with only water, specifically for co-workers who did not like me. One was having so much trouble, they were on the verge of breaking down. They continued to hate me and never knew I was praying for them. As the Lord positioned me, he also sent people to encourage me in that place. You see, I worked in the local county jail, and sometimes it was the inmates that had to encourage me in the Lord.

Although Down for The Count Volume II's chapter, "They Called Me Sarah." dealt with infertility, I didn't go into detail about other struggles. In 2004, I was a victim of the Duke Hydraulic case and began to suffer joint pain and stiffness. I was placed on two medications which were dangerous to my eyes. A year later the Rheumatologist said it wasn't RA.

In 2008, I was hurt in an incident involving a love triangle that clashed in a brawl in front of the jail. Caught in the middle of two women trying to fight each other, I ended up taking the brunt of their blows. My shoulders and neck were injured, a slight tear to the meniscus of my right knee and lower back pain. For a week, I thought I could shake it off and continue working since I was stationed in the control room at the time (the place where officers on light duty were assigned when hurt anyway). But the neck pain was excruciating, so I had to report it. I got a cortisone shot for my knee and tried therapy for my neck.

After going back and forth with Worker's Comp and getting nowhere, I was referred to Aqua therapy which seemed to work for my neck. My therapist said she could tell I had been in a lot of pain because of the condition it was in. She worked on my range of motion and releasing the strain on my neck from where it was compacted, and I felt so much better, but I was released for the third time and decided to manage the pain as best as I could with heating pads and over the counter pain meds. About two years later, I went back to Worker's Comp and ended up suing them. I didn't win because they said I didn't go to my doctor for treatment and blamed my pain on degenerative arthritis. Even my doctor said I didn't have arthritis that wasn't normal for people my age and the Rheumatologist couldn't diagnose Rheumatoid Arthritis. At this point in my career, I had about 20 years of service in, and I decided to return to work and deal with the pain. Eventually, after losing weight, my pain got better, but that was short-lived.

I had to deal with the taunts of others who felt like I wasn't hurt and that I always had an ache or pain somewhere. Well, I did! And being taunted about it started making me think maybe these pains weren't real. It seemed to get worse when I was stressed out, and I began to think back as far as I could to the beginning, tracing the source back to the back injury received during one armed self- defense class in Jail School in 1992. I never reported it to my supervisor because I didn't know about Worker's Comp back then. I just started having severe back spasms and was prescribed muscle relaxers and pain medications. I thought it was due to me being top-heavy, so I eventually had a breast reduction in 1998, which did help take the strain off my back.

In 2017, my Exodus began. You see, I had been in Egypt too long. I began having vertigo, and my doctor suspected I might have had a stroke on the brain or an aneurysm. As they began testing me to rule out these things, the medication I was on caused me to have trouble getting up in the mornings. I would come in late, and because I was temporarily assigned to another area that didn't require me to punch the clock so to speak, I let my supervisor know and told him I was flexing the time I had built up from staying over in courts, which was pretty much every day. The pressure was placed on me from outside antagonists about this, and I was told there was no such thing as "flex" time, and I needed to come to work on time. I was still on medication and suffering headaches and vertigo when I was sent on a three-hour drive alone to pick up an inmate in another county. I prayed as I drove three hours there, picked up a female and drove three hours back with no backup officer and no definitive answer to the cause of the vertigo. Everyone knew of the County directive to send two officers on trips outside the county, but no one cared. I was put in the position to refuse so I could be written up. Many times, I was expected to produce "Bricks without Straw" so to speak, set up to fail. Pushed to the limits and dared to speak up.

The Facebook incident came next, where an employee of another agency of the county took my picture and placed it on Facebook with a derogatory caption. I was in Administration on a coffee break and sat down to drink a cup before Court started. I laid my head back and appeared to be sleeping when the pic was snapped. I was furious because the focus was on the appearance of me asleep and not on the pain it caused me, the embarrassment, and the lack of empathy I received. My co-workers taunted me, and what happened next, I honestly felt like it was intentional, and I felt bad for thinking that.

The door hit me on the left arm, and I walked on to my post. I called the control room to report it because my shoulder started aching, and I knew I would need another shot to calm the pain. I sent an email to my supervisors explaining the previous injury, and I worked the rest of the day and went to Urgent Care after work. The county flat out denied my claim saying the door didn't hit me. A month later, I was hit again, and I let them know it didn't hurt me, but they needed to be careful. I was cursed out in the background. I complained, and nothing was done. Then, a month or so later, they hit me a third time.

God orchestrated these incidents to deliver me from this place. I wanted to stay for three more years, but God said no! He made it, so I had to sue Worker's Comp, and in order to receive my settlement, I had to resign or retire. It was clear. They wanted me gone, so I took early retirement and moved forward. I now know it was all part of God's plan for Pharaoh to let me go. I'm officially out of "Egypt," and I want to encourage you whatever place you are in -dealing with the spirit of Pharaoh, God himself will cause "Pharaoh" to release you. It was God's mighty hand that caused Pharaoh to drive me out!

CHAPTER 4

TINA MOORE

Tina L. Moore was born and raised in Rochester, NY. Tina lives in Rochester with her four children; Shayla, Jeremy, Michael, and Divad and five grandchildren; Kyair, Harlem, Jymere, Jahsier, and Ger'nee. She works in Manufacturing and is the proud owner of TDS Boutique, Yellow Rubies Mentoring Program, and Yellow Gazelle Circle of Empowerment. Tina is also a first time and Best-Selling Author in H.E.R. Extreme Makeover Anthology. She enjoys spending time with her family, writing, and empowering women in their Personal Development and Self Improvement. Tina's hobbies include crocheting, bowling, and designing candy bouquets.

Connect with Tina:

Phone number: 585.448.5566
Email address: info.ygempowerment@gmail.com
Facebook.com/yellowgazelle18
Instagram.com/yellowgazelleempowerment

BENT BUT NOT BROKEN

*She is more precious than rubies; nothing you
desire can compare with her.
Proverbs 3:15
New International Version*

When I think of victory, I think of myself and how I had to reclaim the victory as mine. In a relationship that had recently ended because of stress, exhaustion, a feeling of being drained, and suffering from depression and anxiety. I felt nothing but doubt about myself and my worth. This relationship caused me to feel lost and realizing that I was settling just to say that I was with someone. Things that I wanted for myself, I put on hold just to make sure his needs were met. My eleven-year-old daughter wasn't happy and even displayed actions in school that caused me to question many things about our household state.

On the other hand, I would think she is a child and needed to stay in a child's place because I was fake happy with him. The him from 20 plus years ago. The him who wined and dined me. The him who said he had my back (but really didn't). The him who showed me love or what I thought love was at least. I deserved to be happy, especially after a failed marriage and a failed relationship with a married but separated from his wife man, who he ended up reconciling with. Didn't what I want matter? Didn't I deserve a relationship that I could call my own? I enjoyed the dinners, the gifts, and the date nights with him. He loved me, or at least he said he did. He said he would give me the world, he said, he said, he said. He said a lot and I fell for it.

I believed everything he told me about us. I believed that he loved me but later found out that it was hard for him to love anybody. I believed him to be different from those from my past, and I shared some very intimate things with him. Things that I never shared with anyone else because I trusted him to not hurt me. We had dreams to spend the rest of our lives together. I now know that he was all for himself, and once his mask began to slowly fall off, I still tried to cover our relationship back up. Everything that I worked hard on regarding self-improvement was slowly disappearing, and I was falling into the hands of a narcissist.

My emotional state of mind was in complete turmoil. I wanted to leave him, and I wanted things to work out also. I was so confused because when things were good, they were great, but when things were bad, he made sure I knew that it was all my fault. I was really losing myself at the cost of trying to please someone else, and I apologized each time for being the reason for this or that. What I did or said held no weight. He reigned in this relationship, and there was no room for comparing or competing.

After months of contemplating leaving and ending this relationship, I realized that I had a voice and deserved to be heard. I refused to be treated like I was a piece of coal when I knew that I was a diamond. I started thinking about how far I had come and how hard I worked to get where I am today. I refused to accept his aggressive and narcissistic behavior, and I spoke up for myself. There was no need to inform him how he was going to treat me because he saw nothing wrong in how he treated me. The best thing that I could do for me was to end the relationship.

I asked God to show me, and I prayed over myself and asked to be healed from this. I acknowledged what God was showing me, was obedient, walked away and never looked back. Once I followed God's instructions, better things began to happen for me, and I became aligned with people who meant me good. I had to reintroduce myself to me, and my self-worth became important to me again. I am no longer bound to settle for what doesn't serve me. I am so deserving of love and to be loved by those that know how to love. My healing process included researching and journaling about the failed relationships and how each one was different but so similar. My bounce back involves being an advocate for women who may have experienced the same things that I did and may not have the resources or notion to move on. This experience has inspired me to create a group for women called Ahh-Mazingly Soulful. In this space women are encouraged to affirm themselves daily and to learn how to deal with challenges and struggles that life may throw at us. We will become equipped with how to deal with the challenges head-on and conquer them gracefully.

*If you want something you have never had,
you must be willing to do something
you have never done.*

CHAPTER 5

KIM MALLOY

Kim Malloy is the successful Visionary Entrepreneur Owner of a Cleaning Service / All-natural cleaning product line. Her heart's passion is to become a Transformational motivational speaker. She is on a Divine Journey of living a purpose-driven lifestyle listening to her life and unlocking God's plans for her to shine light towards others.

Kim lost both parents at an early age, was adopted by a family member that was mentally and physically abusive only towards her in the household. Some family members knew about it but never did anything to help her out of the situation. Kim ran away and had no knowledge of self, where she encountered so many disgruntled relationships while looking for love in all the wrong people. She shifted into overload, which led her down a path of self-destruction, but during that, God redirected her heart towards self-discovering the broken mystery pieces of the power within her.

DISCOVERING THE POWER WITHIN

For I know the plans I have for you," declares the
LORD, "plans to prosper you and not to harm you,
plans to give you hope and a future.
Jeremiah 29:11
New International Version

If you are like me, you are thinking I can't go back to my past mistakes and disgruntled relationships that serve no purpose in my life; then you are on the right path through the Divine Crossroads. Continue to stay true to yourself and unlock all the good possibilities that lead you to your purpose. I've learned your purpose is already within. You must reconnect with it. When encountering bad situations acknowledge it as a life lesson and tools gained to keep you focused on your journey to your best self. I am convinced nothing happens accidentally and there's always a reason for everything you experience in life.

On my journey to my best self, I seem to attract manipulators/ social vampires that prey on the fact I have an open and understanding heart. However, I am still working on myself and had a bad past. Honestly, in my opinion, real genuine people are rare to come by. It seems only 10% of people in the world are sincere. Everybody else is hurt; people hurting others for their own pleasure. Maybe I am trying to create a perfect world in my head.

I am learning self-worth, boundaries, and balance on my journey, which is very important to becoming your best self. It may sound simple to a person that hasn't been through a rough childhood, but to me, I was clueless, running away from a mental and physically abusive jack in a box to the reality of the real world. But I am counting it all blessings in disguise! I know I am soaring towards something bigger than myself.

"If you don't know who you are, you will never know
what belongs to you" ~ Dr. Gail Hayes

On this Amazing Journey, I am realizing, "I am the Prize." I am not trying to sound conceited, but I am looking at a better and healthier outlook on my life. The different disgruntled and superficial relationships have taught me a lot about myself, due to me growing up under mental and physical abuse, I learned to tolerate people and situations that didn't have my best interest at heart. My subconscious mind was programmed to not value myself and well- being. I started to listen to my life after questioning myself so much about the fact I didn't fit in with certain people in the world. The fact of the matter is that there are so many lost people in the world. We all are trying to find ourselves in one way or another.

At the time, I didn't realize I was incomplete, looking for love in all the wrong people as well as attracting incomplete people that were on a much lower conscious level; somehow wishing I could fill voids through them. Looking back, it was more like the blind leading the blind. I was attracting people that seemed like they had my best interest on the surface but ended up misleading me in the end. I started giving them labels of trust. During that process, I learned the hard way, "Go Beyond the Surface" to find out people's true intentions towards you.

My present self is quick to say, "I am out!" Just because it seems like the manipulator is heading in a similar direction doesn't mean that they are meant to stay in your life forever, only for a season especially if they don't have loyal traits. On my journey, I experienced that they were headed the opposite way, but there is a soul lesson to learn and implement towards the next life test and move forward. If the relationship isn't encouraging you to become your best version of self, you don't need to continue allowing

people that only want to distract you or use you as a

stepping stone to get what they can from you for the

moment. I am shifting my mindset towards my core

values and morals; I've decided to stand firm even if I

must stand alone.

> "I know where I'm going, and I know the truth, and I
> don't have to be what you want me to be.
> I'm free to be what I want." ~ Muhammad Ali

Flashback reflection: This is a long story without

going into countless episodes. First "Red Flag" going

back to visit my family that didn't help me out of my

mentally abusive jack in the box situation. The year of

2008, I decided to rekindle with some of my

dysfunctional and superficial family members. They

had a surprise birthday party/ sleepover, which was my

first birthday experience with family. Looking back,

they just wanted to expose my emotions so they could

play on them for their own benefits. They realized they couldn't get much from me. Honestly, at that point, I was already sucked dry from the previous relationships. So, they started to act differently towards me. It was almost like they didn't want me around because they weren't able to cash in on the fact of giving me something I never experienced.

The next year came, and it was my birthday again, and not one person said, "Happy Birthday!" That was my second "red flag." I started back going to the church I used to attend years ago. I joined the dance ministry and was going to join the women's outreach ministry, where I thought I would be able to encourage women to live with purpose no matter what life threw at them. My spirit was telling me through encouraging others, I would find my peace and happiness. I didn't know my strength, so I broke down and allowed them to run me away from the church. My point is when you are pursuing something that feels right in the heart, stay still and be firm. Meanwhile if you are feeling alone and hurt, God's got you covered, and it doesn't matter what people think or say.

On your journey, you need to be very focused and be relentless on mastering your life by staying in your lane while unfolding what's in your heart to allow your vision to become a reality. As you know, there will be a lot of twists and turns but don't allow temporary setbacks to offset your course towards your true direction in life. "You may have been knocked down, but not knocked out." I've learned on my journey, God shows up in our weakest moments. Every time we get knocked down by our tribulations, disappointments, heartbreaks, trials we face on a daily basis, as long as we get back up, the fight is not over; only knowledge gained and methods to implement to keep us soaring to our best self.

CREATE AN ACTION MASTER PLAN:

Start where you are now. Balance out the different areas in your life and identify your obstacles. Set positive goals to improve your outcome.

Your Health

Your Finance

Your Social Life

Your Relationships

Your Spiritual Development Life

In life, you have 2 choices either to <u>master your life or stay a victim!</u>

I chose to master my life! Yes, I chose to own every part of my life that was crazy, good and mind-blowing. I owned it all and started to use all the soul lessons I gained from my experiences so far in life to build skills to allow my higher self to dance towards God's Divine plans for my life.

You're probably wondering how I can start listening to my life and unlock God's plans for me?

Allow yourself to be completely honest
with where you are in life

Own It

Stay true to yourself always

Learn to say No to things/ people that don't serve a
positive outlook in your life

Remember everything is a process

Meditate

Take one step at a time, NEVER GIVE UP!

CHAPTER 6

TRENA HINES

Trena Hines is a woman walking this journey in total submission, while seeking God daily with expectations of accelerating to greater heights. She recognizes God as her strength and does not let her circumstances determine her destiny. In the face of adversity, she strives to live a holy and fruitful life, as God officially ordained for her.

Trena's journey and passion is to help others in crisis or as the need presents itself. She is a member of Mount Pleasant Worship and Outreach Center in Raleigh, NC, where she serves on several ministries. Trena is also a member of two community organizations: Women of Triumph and My Sisters Keeper.

She saved the best for last, her greatest asset, she is the mother of Tamarah and Alsalm Hines, grandmother of Jaida, Cairo and Brielle and mother-in-love of Kimberly Hines.

GOD WILL NEVER LEAVE ME
NOR FORSAKE ME

Forsake Me Not, O Lord: O My God,
Be Not Far From Me
Psalm 38:21
King James Version

April 17, 2001, early morning, doing what I usually do. I'm standing at my kitchen sink staring out the window admiring the morning. It had rained hard that night, and it was now a gray day with light rain. I was talking to God in a soft voice asking Him to heal my friend who was in the hospital. I was asking Him to heal her from the sickness that had consumed her body.

And the prayer of faith shall save the sick, and the
Lord shall raise him up; and if he has committed
sins, they shall be forgiven him.
James 5:15

I had gone to the hospital every evening after work for almost 2 weeks to be by her side and be of any assistance she needed. I bathed her and combed her hair. We had conversations about our lives and cultures. She was from Nigeria. I would attentively listen to her as she spoke of her life in her country. She spoke of her walk with Christ. During that time, I wasn't saved, but I attended church. My Nigerian friend was hospitalized because of a goiter, which is an enlarged thyroid gland. The doctor said it developed due to a lack of iodine in her diet. This day, I had decided not to go to the hospital. I received a phone call. It was my friend's roommate. She stated, "It isn't looking good. You need to hurry to the hospital." I immediately ceased everything I was doing and rushed to the hospital. As I'm walking the hall, headed to her room, I passed the Chapel. A strange feeling came over me, which I couldn't explain. I felt the urge to run. So, I ran to her room.

To my surprise the nurse was there, and she told me

my friend had just expired. My heart sank! The

doctors did not mention that death was a possibility.

My friend was gone. I was shocked! How could this

have happened? I felt abandoned due to past losses

of loved ones. I was down for the count. As I sat and

held her hand and talked to that empty vessel, I felt

a great loss.

Precious in the sight of the LORD is the
death of his saints.
Psalm 116:15

Although I felt abandoned, I had peace in knowing

she was in heaven. She was no longer suffering.

While the loss of my friend was still heavy on my

heart, three months later, God took someone else

that was truly dear to me. This was a tremendous

loss to me on top of my Nigerian friend's death.

This person played an important part in my life. This was a person of great wisdom whom I truly admired and loved. This was also a person that loved me unconditionally. This deeply hurt me. I felt so alone knowing this was the last person of that generation to truly love me for me. I got through the homegoing service, which was nice. It was a celebration of life. I thank God for being the wind beneath my wings.

The LORD our God be with us, as he was with our fathers: let him not leave us, nor forsake us. God blessed me through such a trying time.
1 Kings 8:57

Upon returning home from this homegoing, my Nigerian friend's family had genuinely and affectionately thanked me for getting her body home to Nigeria, Africa. The family sent me a videotape of the service. As I was watching the video, my sister/my friend Diane Pace and her daughter Renee had stopped by. I was interested in the cultural service but feeling sad and didn't know I was in the beginning stage of depression. Emotionally, I was broken but didn't know it. Diane talked to me and tried to comfort me, offering encouraging words, but it wasn't working. Mentally I could not be reached at that time. As days passed the gloom was there. I couldn't shake it. I needed to talk, to express my feelings, and share my experience. I realized that I really needed to release the brokenness that had consumed me. The people I needed and wanted had neglected to be there for me. My love and kindness were not reciprocated. I later had a complete meltdown / breakdown. I was down for the count! Oh God I need you now!

For I said in my haste, I am cut off from before thine eyes: nevertheless, thou heardest the voice of my supplications when I cried unto thee.
Psalm 31:22

Feeling abandoned, I became destructive, literally tearing my room apart and crying unmercifully. My womb partners Tamarah and Alsalm witnessed the horror of my pain. They felt helpless and afraid. Their strong tower was now in broken pieces. The woman they knew me to be; the strength, the encourager, their inspiration, the backbone, the go-to person, the glue, the leader, the protector, the provider, the mentor, the mother who only birthed two but was mother hen to many. Unsure of what to do, they called my sister/my friend Marie Hill. She tried to reach me but couldn't assist in the matter. I wasn't hearing her either. I was uncontrollable. During my horror, my sister/my friend Andrea McCullough entered my spirit. I had Marie to call Andrea. She was the one I wanted and felt I needed. I now know that it was God who dropped her in my spirit.

Andrea arrived to find me crouched down on the floor crying uncontrollably. To her shock...Who is this person? She was shocked to see me in that state. She realized that her mouth could not say what she wanted to say. She immediately embraced me and held me tight. I felt the warmth of her love. She began to pray for me, and her prayers brought some comfort.

I have told you these things, so that in Me you may have peace. John 16:33

Although I wasn't a child of God at the time, meaning saved, I was still God's child. I thank God for Andrea's prayers. God spared me from the snares of the enemy. Satan was trying to destroy me.

The thief cometh not, but for to steal, and to kill, and to destroy. I am come that they might have life, and that they might have it more abundantly. John 10:10

EMS was called they were trying to put me in a straitjacket. I remember pleading not to be put in that jacket. They explained that it was for my safety. After arriving at the hospital, my diagnosis was

'Nervous Breakdown.' They wanted to admit me to the psych ward. NO!!! That's not what I needed.

> *Persecuted, but not forsaken; struck down,*
> *but not destroyed.*
> *2 Corinthians 4:9*

I was walking through the valley of the shadow of death. My God was with me, yet I was a sinner. He heard my cry. He heard my sinner's prayer calling for Him to take this hurt from me.

> *In my distress I called upon the LORD and cried*
> *unto my God: he heard my voice out of his temple,*
> *and my cry came before him, even into his ears.*
> *Psalm 18:6*

Some think the strong don't get weak nor weary. The devil is a Liar!!! Yet I knew I didn't need to be admitted to a psych ward. What I needed was a loving ear to listen to me without passing judgment. After calming down and complying with the nursing staff, I agreed to seek individual psychiatric counseling. The doctors had prescribed medication for my anxiety and depression. The 10-day supply of medication they prescribed upon my release that day made my life miserable. I was hallucinating, having nightmares and urinating in the bed. I was a mess! I was down for the count. A couple of weeks later, while visiting at a friend's house, Diane and Renee had stopped by to see me. Shortly afterward, my daughter Tamarah had also stopped by my friend's house, and I told her to run to the pharmacy for the 30-day supply refill of my medications. We all got into a discussion about the medication that I was having refilled. I shared with them about the side effects. With them knowing who I am, adamantly yet lovingly they convinced me that I did not need them. Tamarah truly convinced me with heartfelt words of emotion to not take the medication. I strongly felt compelled to dispose of the prescriptions. I did just that! I knew that God was telling me through those that cared that I didn't need the prescriptions. The void of abandonment was filled.

What the enemy set out to harm me, God said not so! Remember Job? God had to allow Satan to touch him. If Satan could even touch us without God's permission, he would instantly destroy us.

For the LORD thy God will hold thy right hand,
saying unto thee, Fear not, I will be with you.
Isaiah 41:13

My Father said He would never leave me nor forsake me, and His word does not return void. God set me free from depression and anxiety without the medications. Through prayer and words of encouragement from those who cared, I bounced back! God stepped in and blessed me to have peace. He gave me perfect peace.

And the peace of God, which passeth all understanding, shall keep your hearts and minds through Christ Jesus. Philippians 4:7

I was down for the count, but through Christ, I

bounced back. But God!

CHAPTER 7

ANNA LYONS

.

Pastor Anna Lyons is a native of Dallas, Texas. She is the daughter of the late Pastor I. H. Lyons and Dr. Doris J. Lyons. Anna has one son, George Tisdale. She has three grandchildren Jaylen, Jordan and Justyce. She attended Bishop College and received her Master's Degree from Prairie View A.M. University. Anna was an Educator and retired after 32 years of teaching.

Anna currently resides in Durham N.C. and attends Gateway to Heaven United Holy Church. She is the Associate Minister under the leadership of Pastor Marian Freeman-Weaver. Anna is the founder and CEO of Women of Triumph Ministry, Daughters and Sisters of Triumph and Men of Triumph.

Anna is an Independent Business Owner of AmeriPlan Corporation. She is a member of Delta Sigma Theta Sorority and has served in many capacities nationally and locally. Anna also received the Outstanding Church Woman's Award.

FROM THE PALACE TO THE PIT

*No weapon that is formed against thee shall
prosper; and every tongue that shall rise against
thee in judgment thou shalt condemn. This is the
heritage of the servants of the Lord, and their
righteousness is of me, saith the Lord.*
Isaiah 54:17
King James Version

Trials of yesterday are still with us today. Yesterday's

trials and conspiracies are still with us and in many

instances are far worse. People have become bolder

and heartless. Yet as difficult as this may seem we are

called to bear up under the trials that each day brings.

*We must remain steadfast, immovable, always
abounding in the work of the Lord, knowing
that in the Lord, your work is not in vain.*
1 Corinthians 15:18

After being a Pastor's wife for 21 years, a Co-Pastor and

a mother losing my home, my car, and church family,

it was time for me to arise like Deborah of the old. I had

to pick up the warrior mantle for such a time as this. Today across the globe and right in our own backyards, there are enemies on the rampage tearing apart society at every corner. When it came to being first lady and Co-Pastor, I enjoyed it. There were other things that came with the position that I cared not to deal with.

I was born in Dallas, Texas, and I've been in church all my life. My father was a Pastor. Throughout life, I grew up as a Pastor's kid. Church life is all I've ever known. As I got older, I swore I would never marry a Pastor. Well, I did marry a Pastor. We got married and moved to Oklahoma City. It is amazing to look back and see all that the Lord had done in and through our lives in ministry. I loved to walk in on Sunday morning in a sharp suit, designer hats, designer shoes, and a designer purse looking like a fashion model. I would smile while waving and shaking hands like I was Miss America. I couldn't wait to see what God had done through the word and in our ministry. Because I was the daughter of Pastor Ira Lyons and Dr. Doris Lyons, the expectations of me were plenty.

During my time as First Lady, I loved ministering to the women. I was passionate about leading groups. I took great pleasure in seeing other women grow in their relationships with Jesus. I genuinely had a desire to be used by God. But things began to change. As the church grew, so did the demands on me. The more demands, the more stress. It became difficult for me to meet the needs of the church and his personal needs. We got so caught up in the ministry that we lost each other. I felt like I was under a microscope. I had to remind myself that I was not Jesus. Being burned out can easily destroy you and your family. You must take care of yourself. I had to learn to say no to certain things and hope for understanding.

Then all hell broke, and the gossip started. It became very draining to hear individuals who I thought loved us begin to spread rumors about my husband and other women. At first, I ignored it and kept a smile on my face in the public eye. My life became very lonely, they began to distance themselves, and it finally came to an end.

Blessed are you when people insult you, persecute you and falsely say all kinds of evil against you because of me. Rejoice and be glad, because great is your reward in heaven, for in the same way they persecuted the prophets who were before you.
Matthew 5:11-12

In June 2015, I moved to N.C. I was very embarrassed and humiliated as the van pulled up to relocate me. Some of the members stood outside the parsonage watching. Some waved goodbye, some were in tears, and some smiled. It was time. As reality set in, it was now time to take off the mask. I was brought face to face with challenge after challenge. It got to a point I just wanted to quit. A person can only handle something for a short season. But how do I praise Him when my days turn into weeks, my weeks turn into months, my months had turned to years and my years turned into decades? How do I praise Him under the continual pressure? Through all the tests, God allowed me to go through my divorce, addiction to prescription medication, a stroke, heart problems, losing my rental properties, other family problems and going to the bank to withdraw money and there wasn't any. In addition to all of that, I was still expected to preach, prophesy and fulfill my role. The split was amicable, and my divorce was final in 2017.

Even after my divorce, the trials continued. I never saw it coming. The problem no one wants to talk about is an unspoken epidemic among believers. According to a recent report by Barna Research Group, "Born again Christians are just as likely to divorce as are

Non-Christians." I felt like everything I had ever known had been taken from me. My life was vested in my marriage and family. Church was the lens with which I viewed the world. I felt like I was merely surviving and had not yet been given the gift to dream again. The life I had planned, and the vision of my future had disappeared. I had a gut sinking feeling of not knowing what to do or where to go from here. I was truly down for the count.

I was so busy dealing with the daily rollercoaster of emotions and figuring out my finances. I had forgotten to do one thing ...ask God what is the next chapter in my life. I had to step back and ask, "What is my new vision now that I'm divorced and over 50?" What plan does God have for my life? Identifying that vision became my new goal. It was time for me to dust myself off and move forward. I had to realize there is nothing too hard for my God. And with His help, I can do whatever I put my mind to.

I can do all things through Christ
who strengthens me.
Philippians 4:13

I wanted to feel confident again. That's when I began my new teaching job. I asked God to send me to a church home. That's when things began to change for the better. I joined Gateway to Heaven United Holy Church, under the leadership of the late Mae V. Horne. God began to restore me and make me whole again.

But seek first his kingdom and his righteousness, and
all these things will be given to you as well.
Matthew 6:33

In 2016, I realized quickly the philosophy of the whys behind my pain. It had been prophesied years ago that I would have a Women's Ministry.

*For I know the plans I have for you," declares the
LORD, "plans to prosper you and not to harm you,
plans to give you hope and a future.*
Jeremiah 29:11

God blessed me to bring that prophecy to life. I began
spending time organizing my Women's Ministry. This
was the best decision I had ever made. From my
ministry experience, I had seen many women who were
hurting like me. Some were going through a divorce,
health-related issues, mental health, sexual abuse,
drug addiction, etc. So, I took a leap of faith and birthed
The Women of Triumph Ministry. I would gather the
women for a prayer breakfast, and that's when the
transformation began.

God's standard for restoration is much higher. God's
goal is to restore every person for his original intent for
their life.

All have sinned and fallen short of the glory of God.
Romans 3:23"

God healed my body and restored me to divine health. He restored my finances to a state of heavenly abundance. He redeemed my mind from depression and fear. He restored my state of power, love, and a sound mind. Thank God he delivered me from sin and restored me. I'm free to walk before Him in holiness and purity. Through the love of God, I was able to bounce back from life's blows. I pray that my testimony blesses someone that is going through a rough time. Just know that God can do all but fail.

If you are longing to recover lost years and relationships, hurt feelings or have been separated from God, you need to know that God will restore you. Don't be stuck. Break out of your past into God's future. God loves you. Amen!!!

CHAPTER 8

CONSTANCE HARRIS

Elder Constance Harris, a native of Greenville, NC, resides in Durham, NC. Elder Harris is a member of Gateway to Heaven United Holy Church of America. She is the Southern Central District's Youth Department Chairperson. She was ordained as an Elder in September 2018.

Elder Constance Harris is also a part of the Women of Triumph Ministries, under the leadership of Elder Anna Lyons. She works full time as a Credit and Collections Analyst.

Elder Harris is a June 2017 graduate of United Christian College-Durham extension where she graduated Cum Laude with an Associate's Degree in Biblical Studies, and she is a 1990 graduate of East Carolina University. She has been married since 1995 to Elder John Harris and has three adult children.

Connect with Constance:

Email: cwharris1968@gmail.com
www.Facebook.com/constance.harris3
Instagram: constance1968

A BRIGHT FUTURE IN THE MIDST OF DARKNESS

For I know the thoughts that I think toward you, saith the Lord, thoughts of peace, and not of evil, to give you an expected end. Jeremiah 29:11 King James Version

Well, what can I say but to God be the Glory for all He's done for me! The scripture, Jeremiah 29:11, holds a personal meaning for me because when I think back on my life, I never thought I would be where I am today.

I was a much-loved child growing up in a home with two caring parents who made sure I had all I needed. I also grew up with two great extended families with cousins, aunt, uncles and grandmothers. I was very trusting of others and didn't see anything wrong with my growing relationship with my maternal grandmother's boyfriend, who I will name Ray for this piece. I was certainly curious about the special attention he gave me when we were alone. The caresses and smiles that Ray gave me made me think in my 7-year-old mind that I was just someone special. The unfortunate side is that it made me think it was okay to allow someone to be physically close to me. I am grateful, however that the special attention never escalated to more than inappropriate touches. Once I reached an age of around 12, I realized that Ray was taking advantage of me and I began to see him as the nasty old man he was. One day, when he approached me for the final time, I told him to leave me alone with so much disdain in my voice that he never bothered me again, but sadly the damage had already been done.

As I grew into a teenager, I exhibited an unhealthy fascination of the opposite sex that was a byproduct of the molestation of my younger years. I thought that if a boy didn't like me that I wasn't worth anything. I would often cross the line of what a good girl should allow a boyfriend to do in order to keep their attention. I thought this type of behavior was ok and that everyone my age was doing it. I was young and naïve. You might think that I wasn't getting any advice from anyone about not getting involved with sex and what it led to. The problem was I got the advice much later than I should have. That lustful spirit had taken hold of me, and I didn't know how to get rid of it. Attending church didn't help me as I was a member of the Catholic Church that never addressed matters like that. I listened to R&B music, like most African American teenagers, with lyrics about sex and having a good time. I remember Marvin Gaye's song "Sexual Healing" being a favorite of mine in the 9th grade. If only I knew then what I know now about the dangers of sex before marriage. It did eventually lead to an unwanted pregnancy and an abortion while in high school. My parents were not about to allow a baby in the household, and I was too scared to argue against their decision. That abortion was a defining moment in my teen years. One Sunday, I sat in the church chapel one day before service and asked God to forgive me for what I had done. I had contemplated suicide and felt really lost. I remember clearly sitting on the pew and feeling the presence of something around me that made the hair sit upon my neck. It scared me to the core. I wanted to run out of the church as tears welled up in my eyes, but I continued to sit realizing that God's presence was with me letting me know that everything would be okay and that he had good plans for me. I knew nothing about the Bible during those times of my life, but I believed that God was real and that he was looking out for me.

As I later entered college, I focused on schoolwork and was a great student. Unfortunately, I carried the bad habits concerning men into college. I did have a steady boyfriend while in college, but that didn't stop me from sampling the masculine treats on campus from time to time. I did graduate on time and married my long-time boyfriend at age 22. It seemed like the right thing to do. After all, I had to escape from the house of my parents where I'd managed to hide most of my dirt from them for so many years. My marriage didn't go so well with my demons catching up with me as I allowed guys to catch my eye. Once I knew the marriage wasn't working, I went back to my old ways. Life is funny though because, in the midst of the old habits and bad choices, God sent a reminder of his faithfulness to me. I had a relationship with a Pastor who introduced me to Jesus by bringing me to the Pentecostal church with him. He was in the midst of divorce himself, and I guess when he finally came to himself, he knew I wasn't the right woman for him. We were both distractions for each other during divorces, and in the end, he told me we were unequally yoked. I didn't totally understand it at the time. All I knew was that he broke up with me and I was devastated. The pain I felt was unbearable, so I distracted myself again with men and happy hours at bars after work with girlfriends. I had fallen into depression and a lack of love for anyone.

After being in a low-place for a long time, God intervened and allowed someone to come into my life that would change my life forever – a baby. I was scared, but I knew so many women before me, had babies as single-mothers and wasn't going to allow my mistakes to end another baby's life. My daughter, Cierra, was born in May 1993 and my life was never the same. I loved my daughter unconditionally and having her in my life began the healing in my life. While her father didn't want to be in her life, I knew God was with us, and everything would be ok. Once the haze of troubles and hurt lifted I began to pray for God to forgive me for my sins and to help me to be a good person and mother to my daughter. I had a great support system with my parents and life was good. I knew that my life wasn't to stay that way. I wanted to be married, and I wanted a father for my daughter. I grew up in a two-parent home, and I wanted that for my daughter. I had met men from time-to-time but none that God wanted me to be with. I refused to allow my daughter to see me with a rotating door of men. So, I waited for God to send me the man to marry.

To God be the glory because I really didn't have to wait long. I was introduced to John Harris in February 1994, by a mutual friend. We talked on the phone for two weeks before physically seeing each other. We developed a respect for each other than transcended what we looked like. When we finally got to see each other, we knew it was a match in Heaven. We married in September 1995, and God has been blessing us ever since. Now we haven't been without test and trials, but God has gotten us through every single one of them. We were blessed with two sons, Michael and Trey, and John eventually adopted Cierra and made her officially his daughter. We were later called into ministry and were both ordained as Elders in the United Holy Church of America in 2018. God surely had good thoughts for me, and a future filled with hope and blessings.

CHAPTER 9

VISIONARY FELICIA C. LUCAS

Minister Felicia C. Lucas is a #1 International Bestselling Author, 9-time Bestselling Author, Speaker, Coach, Event Planner and Book Publisher. In 2001, Felicia and her husband, Pastor Kelvin Lucas, founded *Take It By Force Ministries*, Inc. a non-profit 501 © 3 organization and in 2003 became the founders/ Senior Leadership at *Dominion Tabernacle Church*. They were married in 1997 and have three children, Isaiah, Kelsey and Silas.

Felicia also known as "The Publishing Chick" ™ is the CEO of *His Glory Creations Publishing, LLC* and owner of *His Glory Creations Christian Store*. She is a graduate of the University of North Carolina at Chapel Hill where she received a Bachelor of Arts in Speech Communication. For over 24 years she has worked in the Human Resources field.

Connect with Felicia:

www.felicialucas.com

www.hisglorycreations.com

Facebook: HGCPAC

Facebook: Author and Speaker Felicia Lucas

Instagram: Coach Felicia Lucas

Twitter: MoveToYourBestU

Other literary works by Felicia C. Lucas:

- Make it Happen: Moving Towards Your Best U!
- Get in the Game: A Teen's Playbook for Winning the Game of Life
- The Bounce Back: Triumphant Stories of Resiliency and Perseverance
- Invitation to Intimacy
- Down for the Count: Bouncing Back from Life's Blows-Volumes I and II
- Affirmations that Remind Me (Marilyn Porter)
- 100 Inspiring Words (Marilyn Porter)
- ABC's of Authorship
- Entrepreneurial Elevation (Cheryl Wood)
- Stuff: A Collection of Middle Schools Thoughts-Volumes I and II

A VOICE CRYING OUT IN SILENCE

But you are a chosen people, a royal priesthood, a holy nation, God's special possession, that you may declare the praises of him who called you out of darkness into his wonderful light.
1 Peter 2: 9
New International Version

Do you know what is the 2nd leading cause of death among college students and the 3rd leading cause of death among youth between the ages of 15-24? The rate of U.S. adolescents and young adults dying of suicide has reached its highest level in nearly two decades, according to the Journal of the American Medical Association. In 2017, there were 47 percent more suicides among people aged 15 to 19 than in the year 2000. Overall, there are 36 percent more people aged 20 to 24 living in the U.S. today than at the turn of the century. With more than 6,200 suicides among people aged 15 to 24, suicide ranked as the second-leading cause of death for people in that age group in 2017, trailing behind deaths from unintentional motor vehicle accidents.

According to the Mayo Clinic: "Suicidal thoughts have numerous causes, according to the Mayo Clinic. Most often, suicidal thoughts are the result of feeling like you can't cope

when you're faced with what seems to be an overwhelming life situation. If you don't have hope for the future, you may mistakenly think suicide is a solution. You may experience a sort of tunnel vision, wherein the middle of a crisis, you believe suicide is the only way out. According to the article, Psychologists point to several reasons why people commit suicide, from depression to psychosis to stressful life situations. But one thing is certain: Whatever drives someone to take their own life ultimately begins in the mind. Suicidal thoughts precede suicide. As it turns out, suicidal thoughts are not uncommon. Nearly 8.3 million adults age 18 and older in the United States—that's 3.7 percent—had serious thoughts of suicide in the past year, according to a study called "Suicidal Thoughts and Behaviors Among Adults > 18 Years" released by the Centers for Disease Control and Prevention. Although some suicides are impulsive, most are planned out. More than 2 million adult Americans made a suicide plan in the past year, and about half that many went through with the plan."

I will never forget my freshman year at the University of North Carolina at Chapel Hill, when I received a call that one of the youths in the community back home, 8 years old, had killed himself. I remember driving home, thinking about how this could have happened. The event devastated the local church community and changed the dynamics of his household. He had left a note for his parents to share the reason for his actions. He expressed that he felt that they spent more time at church rather than with him. He was convinced that ending his life was the best option and that death would bring the desired end to his hurting situation.

Have you ever felt that way? There was a point in which I felt that no one wanted me, that no one loved me and that no one needed me. I felt like I was invisible. I didn't matter and that I was not good enough. I was stressed to the max and felt so lost and insignificant. I remember standing in my bedroom feeling so alone, even though there were others in the house. I quietly went into the bathroom, opened the medicine cabinet, grabbed a bottle of pills, went back into my bedroom and stood in front of my mirror and said, "God, if I wake up in the morning, then I am meant to live but if I don't then my life is meant to be over." I took more than the recommended dose of the pills and went to sleep....and thank God; my life was not meant to be over because I am still here today!

How did I end up at that point in life where I felt that I had no purpose or reason to exist? From the outside, everything looked like it was going well, but on the inside, I was broken, bruised and so unfulfilled. It was those silent cries for help that no one heard, and therefore they could not help me. I often think about the "what ifs". What if I had not survived the suicidal attempt? I would not be the wife, mother, minister, mentor, publisher, entrepreneur, author, or speaker that I have become. I would not have had the chance to inspire so many others to write and share their story. Just like me, there are so many other adults who carry deep, dark secrets of things they have experienced in life that writing and sharing about it, becomes a part of someone else's breakthrough. Many people see me now, and the numerous accomplishments that I have obtained but little do they know that I have carried pain, rejection, betrayal, depression, worthlessness and hopelessness inside, but now I am liberated and capable of living my best life yet! As I share my experiences, it gives me an opportunity to impact and inspire others to pursue their God-given destiny!

If you or someone you know is having suicidal thoughts, there is a resource that is available for you:

The National Suicide Prevention Lifeline provides free and confidential emotional support to people in suicidal crisis or emotional distress 24 hours a day, 7 days a week, across the United States. The Lifeline is comprised of a national network of over 150 local crisis centers, combining custom local care and resources with national standards and best practices.

NATIONAL SUICIDE PREVENTION LIFELINE

1-800-273-TALK

www.suicidepreventionlifeline.org

Crisis Text Line is free, 24/7 support for those in crisis. Text 741741 from anywhere in the US to text with a trained Crisis Counselor. Crisis Text Line trains volunteers to support people in crisis.

CRISIS TEXT LINE |

Maybe you can't relate to an individual that has had suicidal thoughts. But maybe you can identify with Spiritual Suicide. Spiritual Suicide is a point in which we die in producing God's kingdom on the earth.

And God blessed them, and God said unto them, Be
fruitful, and multiply, and replenish the earth, and
subdue it: and have dominion over the fish of the sea,
and over the fowl of the air, and over every living
thing that moveth upon the earth.
Genesis 1:28

God desires us to be productive and to advance His

kingdom on the earth. We must not stop producing

what God has said. We can't allow our dreams to die! If

God ordained it, it must come forth. He is calling us to

Him. We can't allow circumstances, people, things or

anything to kill us or the dreams that are within us. The

vision can't stop; it can't die now! We can't die now!

There are souls that need us to produce God's glory in

the earth despite the cost. It must be about God and not

about us!

Even in my natural suicide attempt, God had

another plan! I could not die at that point in my life

because he had a destiny for me, a purpose in which I

continue to fulfill. No one had really spoken to me about God's plan and my destiny in him. Some of the advice I had received was *"Sticks and Stones may break your bones, but words can never hurt!"* That is the biggest lie ever told. Words do hurt, and life hurts, but how we choose to deal with our lives will determine if we walk into our destiny and get all that God has for us. **YOU CAN'T DIE NOW! GOD IS CALLING YOUR NAME AND DESIRING FOR YOU TO DO HIS WILL.** He wants us to be fruitful, productive, produce excellence and faithful unto him. God has a plan. You are not an accident! Seek Him for His Plan and begin to walk in it!

His Glory Creations Publishing, LLC is an International Christian Book Publishing Company, which provides publishing services for clients. They help launch and scale the creative works of new, aspiring and seasoned authors across the globe, through stories that are inspirational, empowering, life-changing or educational in nature, including fiction and non-fiction.

DESIRE TO KNOW MORE?
CONTACT INFORMATION

CEO/Founder: Felicia C. Lucas

Website: www.hisglorycreationspublishing.com

Email: hgcpublishingllc@gmail.com

Phone: 919-679-1706

www.ingramcontent.com/pod-product-compliance
Lightning Source LLC
LaVergne TN
LVHW051419080426
835508LV00022B/3153